Something

Understood

Something
Understood

Softness and peace, and joy, and love, and bliss
Exalted manna, gladness of the best,
Heaven in ordinary, man well dressed,
The Milky Way, the bird of Paradise,

Church bells beyond the stars heard , the soul's blood,
The land of spices; something understood.
                                        "Prayer"
                                 George Herbert

Every Other Thursday Press · Cambridge, Massachusetts

Library of Congress Catalog Card Number: 95-74762

ISBN 0-9619960-4-8

Copyright 1996 by Every Other Thursday Press

First Edition
Printed in the United States of America

Book Design/Desktop Publisher: Marie Louise St. Onge
Printer: Puritan Press
Cover Art: Maria Lindberg "A Doorway in Rhodes, Greece"
          from a photograph by Thomas Melone

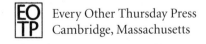 Every Other Thursday Press
Cambridge, Massachusetts

ACKNOWLEDGMENTS

AD HOC MONADNOCK ~ A LITERARY ANTHOLOGY: *Naked Bread*
Skinnydipping

COLLEGE ENGLISH: *After I Quit Drinking*

FIELD: *Evening Hemlocks*
Light-struck

MASSACHUSETTS REVIEW: *Stopping the Jesus*

MIDLAND REVIEW: *Postcard From New Hampshire*

NIMROD: *Calling to the Soul of My Unborn Child*

PALANQUIN PRESS: *The Bricklayers*

SOJOURNER: *Sea Window*

SOUNDINGS EAST: *Note to an Ancestor*

SOUTHERN POETRY REVIEW: *Silence*

THE BRIDGE: *The Bench*

THE SUN: *This Day*

WHISKEY ISLAND REVIEW: *My Father Swearing*

YANKEE: *For Sidonie-Gabrielle Collette*

CONTRIBUTORS

BONNIE BISHOP
POLLY BROWN
SUSAN DONNELLY
JOHN HILDEBIDLE
JOHN HODGEN
BILL HOLSHOUSER
ADELLE LEIBLEIN
DEBORAH MELONE
NORA MITCHELL
VALERY NASH
CON SQUIRES
PRISCILLA WEBSTER WILLIAMS

TABLE OF CONTENTS

Acknowledgments v
Introduction xi

BONNIE BISHOP
Postcard from New Hampshire 3
At The Ipswich River Sanctuary 4
College 6
On Seeing a Photo from the War in the Former Yugoslavia 8
Swimming in the Rain 10

POLLY BROWN
White Chairs at 22 Wood Street 11
Cleaning the Ceiling 12
For Dana 14
About physics, about the weather, about love 16

SUSAN DONNELLY
Men of Ireland: A Photograph 18
The Redhaired Mail Carrier 20
The Bricklayers 21
A Sweater 22
Lunch Break on Moody Street 23

JOHN HILDEBIDLE
A Little Time to Myself 24
Herzegovina 25
Imogen and Twinka at Yosemite 26
Mocker 27
There 28

JOHN HODGEN
For a Friend, Gone for a Year to Galway 30
Man Tosses Body from Fourth Floor 31
Stopping the Jesus 32
This Day 33
My Father Swearing 34

BILL HOLSHOUSER
The Kingfisher 35
Silence 36
Naked Bread 38
Finding Your Voice 39
Skinnydipping 40

ADELLE LEIBLEIN
Calling to the Soul of My Unborn Child   42
On Recalling the Name of a Woman   44
Just   46

DEBORAH MELONE
The Simplest Things   47
Snowball's Chance   48
On Finding Four-Leaf Clovers   50
The Optics of Speech   51
Call Waiting   52

NORA MITCHELL
After I Quit Drinking   53
What Comes Next   54
Teddy Roosevelt in Cuba   56
Learning to Sing   58
Everything and Nothing   59

VALERY NASH
The Bench   60
The Evening Hemlocks   62
Sea Window   63
Light-Struck   64
For Sidonie-Gabrielle Colette   66

CON SQUIRES
The Thief Wu Wei Pleads for His Hand   67
On First Encountering Zimmer's Poems
    While Drinking Decaf Behind the Deli at 10:10AM
    and Experiencing the Clarification
    of a Substantial Hangover and Remembering
    That I Was Recently Mistaken for Zimmer
    Three Times in One Exciting Day   70

PRISCILLA WEBSTER WILLIAMS
Unnamed   72
Foster Child   73
Skating at Night on Swanzey Lake   74
Brazil   75
Note to an Ancestor   76

CONTRIBUTORS' NOTES   78

INTRODUCTION

There are so many ways to write this introduction. It could start with me, who began Every Other Thursday in 1980. I chose people whose work I admired from the classes I'd taken, or sometimes, as in the case of Nora Mitchell, from a single poem I read in a new magazine. For two years the group met on alternate Thursdays at my house; now we take turns. I tried in those early years to provide continuity within a very loose formal structure, on the hunch that the center had better hold on its own.

I began, I chose, I tried ... at this point the first person pronoun gets to me and I put the pencil down. How relatively easy writing a poem seems! When your goal is always to open the heart, enter the I. You hope to surprise yourself and others by uncovering some hidden part of yourself: your own eccentricity of language, stubbornness of vision, particular panache in the whole carefree tightrope act.

So tear off the page and take another approach. In this, a group of near strangers enters a room, each carrying a poem. Years pass: the group membership changes a little; individuals age and develop; the poems strengthen. Somehow, as they lovingly scrutinize a poem about a happy or a traumatic life event, as they focus only on the poem, the strangers begin to comfort and encourage, become part of that life event. They even begin to breathe differently as they settle into a poetry evening and look around. One night, nearly fifteen years later — on a different night for each — they realize this neutral group of amiable poets has become a group of close friends, joined in poetry.

But all this is still not quite enough, and the writer of introductions shuts her eyes. She sees moonlit shadows on snow, as she is summoned across a Vermont yard to a phone, to learn of the chosen name for our first anthology. "And Susan," cries Erika, "You *must* like it!" (Possible names had pursued us for months, gathered by Erika Mumford from her hospital bed.) Indeed, at the heart of any words about Every Other Thursday is another picture: that of Erika, IV in arm, conducting a workshop in her bedroom in the last weeks of her life. "Tell me," she asked us once, "Am I writing *too* much about cancer, do you think?"

Then there's a snapshot of John H. and John H. cheering the Pawtucket Red Sox from the bleachers at a farm team game. Bonnie, noting shore birds off Nahant. Adelle, lover of intricacies, who shapes visual art as she writes a family portrait gallery. Priscilla, spinning a name. Bill, with a famous head cold, and riding a notorious horse. Deborah, with her fractals, poems in puzzles, her wealth of four-leaf-clovers. There are Polly's two white lawn chairs, from whose calm symmetry she is torn by a student's death. Con on a business flight, entering a new poem into his laptop. The night Susan brought her whole life in a poem to the group and, trembling, asked to go first. The season Valery's vision faltered, giving her insights into light and darkness that have entered and deepened her poems.

Arrival of Susannah. Arrival of Aidan. Marriage of Con and Bonnie. The Hodgen father and daughter writing awards. Departure of Phyllis, a strong participant for years. Moves: Nora to Burlington, Adelle to Nashua. The list could continue, but it must stop here, because an introduction is like a poem. Too many facts will mar it: true feeling and craft are all it can offer. That's something this writer begins to understand at last, as she concludes. As she offers, simply and with love, this book to its readers.

SUSAN DONNELLY

Something

Understood

POSTCARD FROM NEW HAMPSHIRE

Bonnie Bishop

I came here to get away,
in the morning decide on a walk.
A cold tapestry — limb and bole,
snow, boulders and their skirts
of star moss — closes in
around the road to a cemetery

glazed with ice. Among the family
plots so many children: names enough
to fill a tall tablet, ages
numbered to the very month and day.
I think we drop into flesh
from the lake of spirit.
At its margin, the recent dead

and those waiting to be born
mill about in the mist;
an old man caresses his grandchild
before each is drawn away

one to surrender self, the other
to seek it. At the inn,
stenciled flowers climb
an invisible trellis.

I warm my feet at the fire
and break open pumpkin muffins
as orange as topaz. There
is no getting away.

AT THE IPSWICH RIVER SANCTUARY

Bonnie Bishop

—for David and Gene

In early December
when you can see again
how it is with the trees,

how they have been quietly
extending themselves
under the summer leaves,

we followed friends
into the woods.
Our pockets were bulging

with sunflower seeds.
Our friends knew where to stop
and taught us how to stand

with arms outstretched
hands full of seeds.
A chickadee from the gray

depths came quickly,
touched my thumb
with his nervous, curving feet,

paused to sort the seeds,
chose one
and flickered off, quick as blinking.

When we walked on,
birds followed us.
We stopped

again to invite
the weightless wing,
to learn

by standing still
how we may,
ourselves, extend.

COLLEGE

Bonnie Bishop

Seventeen, and one night
after the library closed,
I walked downhill
where the sidewalk peters out

and farms begin. In the gathering
leaves on Pearl Street,
old roots broke out
of the pavement. On the
breeze from the west
I could smell fields,

cows standing in the night.
I had never felt so alone
and far from home, ·

so full of possibility.
On Prospect, a house
like the others —

porch to the street
white clapboard
and black shutters,
pumpkin on the step
rippled windows
(six over six)

and the shades drawn.
Behind the luminous squares,

hands new to the task
repeated ascending scales.
I stood still
in the dark soft air

as time lifted
like the curtain
on opening night,
my skin gone
to glass, and glowing.

ON SEEING A PHOTO FROM THE WAR
IN THE FORMER YUGOSLAVIA

Bonnie Bishop

In June, 1970, I left Athens heading north
in a VW van with Don, a Vietnam vet
who had come to Greece from Asia, overland.
Three other guys and one girl traveled
with us; everyone had sleeping bags,
knapsacks, long hair. Don, on speed,
drove all night, hunched furiously
over the steering wheel, through Macedonia
over a spine of mountains while wisps
of fog bashed the windshield.

I must have been asleep when we crossed
the border. At dawn, we came down
into Dubrovnik and parked on a
stone terrace overlooking the Adriatic.
The morning was soft and the sea foggy.
I went to buy bread and coffee.
Few people were stirring. We brewed
the coffee cowboy style, grounds
in the pot, and drank it with extra
sugar. After breakfast, Don slept
while one of the other guys drove. By noon
we were deep in farm country, wheat fields,
vegetable patches, stone walls.
We stopped in a village. A pack

of children followed us to a bakery,
their eyes wide at our strange appearance.
Their small hands reached out to pat
our clothes, our hair, our faces.
I gave my earrings to a little girl.
We bought round crusty loaves.

The children watched us eat, waved
sadly as we drove away. This could have
been Bosnia, but in those days,
I didn't read the map. We were heading
for Annette, in Munich. She
said we could stay with her.

In the afternoon, we began to climb
into mountains. The road grew
narrow and twisty, the terrain wild —
deep ravines, rock outcroppings.
The old van was laboring but
no one was in a hurry.
Then, in front of us, an ox cart —
huge wooden wheels grinding
up the slope, the shoulders
of the oxen rippling like grass
in the wind. On the cart a family
of gypsies; the father drove,
mother beside him, baby on her lap,
son walking, and a young girl
set among painted boxes, swinging her feet
off the back. She stared at us and
we stared back, impassive,
as we made our separate journeys.

Just before the summit they turned
into the woods. We descended
to a plain of fields and orchards.
In late afternoon, Don pulled off
by a lane that led through two rows of trees
to a stone house in an orchard.
He walked down the lane to ask
permission to camp. We set up
the cook stove, made a stew
of carrots, apples, onions and potatoes.
The night was clear and cool. In the dark
the boughs of the apple trees made black
rivers through the stars. After we ate,
Don went back to the farmhouse
to drink with our host, and in the morning
told us they'd talked all night about the war.
Next day, we drove to the Austrian border.

SWIMMING IN THE RAIN

BONNIE BISHOP

last day of vacation in the mountains
swimming in the rain
I forget Michelle whose boyfriend
shot her in the eye and Joey in jail
for throwing dynamite   really   I haven't
given them one thought all week they
are not stories but kids I used to
sit down with   I just go
swimming   the rain makes
swelling circles on the lake   I round
the dock   the loon stops paddling
looks at me   I see his dense
black head   the fine black and white
configuration of feathers on his back
he looks away   he dips his beak
the white ring on his neck
arches like a tiny bridge   he is
so close and not afraid   I am
only afraid to frighten him
have I let them down
forgetting   the whole time
I don't know any more
than the wild bird does why
I bring violence to the lake
bring wildness home

WHITE CHAIRS AT 22 WOOD STREET

POLLY BROWN

I bought them just before
the fire, wanting after all these years
a way to sit comfortably
out in the air,

so when I started to faint
pacing there by the forsythia
that's where they put me —
in a white chair, in our neighbor's shade.

But I can sit in them without
remembering that,
or holding against them
how ugly they are. Unlike wooden chairs

they handle the slope of our lawn:
plant their feet in the roots of the grass,
straddle, and adjust: a herd
of white resin plastic mountain goats;

and since they're easy to lift
we haul them all over, following
the light we want: under the spruce out back,
by the maple, or enthroned

for the prime vista towards the west.
When we hurry away, leaving them odd
and alone, each chair holds the way it feels
to sit in that place. Ghosts

come and use them. Now, for example,
Mrs. Whitton, who lived here before us,
rests from weeding, waves
a gentle, dismissive hand.

CLEANING THE CEILING

POLLY BROWN

On scaffolding lifted high
in the chapel's heaven,
Pier Giorgio Bonetti sponges away
centuries of Rome's dust, the residue

of Greek wine used as cleaning solvent
by earlier conservators,
varnishes made of animal glues, soot
from tallow candles burning below.

Gradually sibyls and ancestors of Christ
appear pink-and-salmon-fleshed,
in morning light.
The weather on the day of Creation improves.

And a crowd of experts leans to watch
as Bonetti finds a hair, then another hair
— "Michaelangelo worked on this section
with an old brush" —

and then a cluster, a constellation
of thumbprints
checking the set of the intonato.
"You see —

Bonetti and the Master, side by side,
labor together to give us the masterpiece."
The experts chuckle.
Bonetti sponges in more sun.

And in time God's own face emerges
from the gloom.
In a rare hour between observers —
when the Japanese cinematographer has fallen asleep —

like a customer to his barber
God confides to Bonetti: "All work of creation
uncovers the past.
The Universe," he says,

"was a folded flower in the dust after a party,
to which I added water."
Bonetti nods,
remembering parties of his own.

Then he rubs his eyes,
a stiffness in his neck —
the Japanese cinematographer startles, yawns —
and God is mere fresco again,

and Bonetti himself
well-paid for an unusual form
of housework. The height, he decides,
dizziness,

lets each of us think that by reaching out a hand
we can begin those miracles
again. And his miracle stretches
and reaches a hand back.

FOR DANA

POLLY BROWN

i

In the middle of our unit on flight
one of my students, without warning,
took wing. Propelled by the van
which had hit her a second before,
bearing a few broken bones, but with her vision
perhaps still intact, she traveled
in an arc through rain and fog
and darkness, and landed faraway
in the street. Her sister, who had just stepped back,
could not see her path; the driver of the van
still struggled for control. A friend
of her mother's, by chance nearby,
saw her land, saw the blood rise
suddenly into her mouth.

ii

They were on their way to the movies.
I consider a campaign against movies.

They were crossing the street.
I consider a campaign against streets, against drivers.

They were only children. I settle
on a campaign against children:

all of them, all of them
should stop their foolishness,

make the sense we need,
grow up right now.

iii

In my image of her she has one hand
clapped over her mouth, having spoken again
out of turn or too soon. Such vividness
runs into penalties — it's true —

but I loved her lack of subterfuge,
ardent speech, quick laughter.
When I quiet the class, two months later,
hers is one of the last voices speaking, still.

iv

Latest and youngest ghost,
you travel with me now,
with others I've lost.
In the strange heaven, the full
tour bus of my heart,
you craft shrewd games of cribbage
against my grandmother;
you and David, my friend,
arguing late at night,
have world affairs
nearly straightened out.

On the radio,
somebody still hasn't found
what he's looking for,
and I notice you listening,
watching the world through my eyes.
What would you seek through me?
Whatever it is, I am happy
to carry you there,
knowing it must be somehow
on my way.

ABOUT PHYSICS, ABOUT THE WEATHER, ABOUT LOVE

Polly Brown

Cold air weighs more than warm.
Under the skylight, lying
in bed, I feel a stream of cold
falling in from the sky

like the cold air sliding down
over Coddington Road, evenings in late fall
when we bundled into the truck
and went for rides: blackbird highways,

deer grazing, once an owl
swooping out of the woods above
to an apple orchard below, and our own small
animal child between us

blinking and blinking to stay awake.
Coddington terraced the long hill
halfway up its height, and you said if we opened
the windows and drove slow

we could feel as we crossed them
the currents of cold air
following the hill's folds
to the valley, filling it with frost:

carrying (I said) the view from the hill's top
to a pattern of stars on black stones
by Seven Mile Creek. Those conversations
carried us home, and here:

here the town's above us, the woods and swamp
below; here the wide-eyed child has grown
and gone away. The cold, if it has
a name at all, is her absence, necessary,

awkward. But we ford that chilly river,
we still do our best learning — about physics,
about the weather, about love —
side by side.

MEN OF IRELAND: A PHOTOGRAPH

Susan Donnelly

Before three doorways
stand four men I've known always.
They greet each other,
bandy the odd anecdote
abroad in the village air.

The quick of a joke
rides the harsh lines on each face.
Labor has scored them,
bent the back of the oldest —
toothless, with his high cackle.

The young boy's narrow
wrists show from his cord jacket.
Not very bold yet,
he listens, smiles, blushes,
his cheek soft as a hedge rose.

I used to languish
over men like the dark one,
"black Irish." Jocko
Clougherty, for example,
a flask in his back pocket.

And the blond farmer,
that twist to his mouth recalls
the paranoia
and the sorrowful wit
of my boss in the newsroom.

They'd nod if I spoke,
tip their caps and a strangeness
would come over us
all, abashed by both shores
of the dividing ocean,

close as they feel now,
in race-knowledge, intimate:
those ruddy cheekbones;
thick hair; the sunken,
used grey face of my father.

THE REDHAIRED MAIL CARRIER

Susan Donnelly

This time of year, it's the color
of the leaves she tramples, tilted
with the weight of the mailbag.
She's in postal blue, but curls
bounce raucous behind her.
She doesn't waste time, wears
an eagle on her arm, looks nineteen

but is probably older. She's got
somewhere else she wants to return to,
so she's brisk, bringing catalogs full
of the trumpery of riches,
sometimes a love letter. Delivers that
the same way she does bills: neat,
with a clang of the metal slot.

Then she's off again, hitching one shoulder.

THE BRICKLAYERS

Susan Donnelly

The bedspread
patterns my face
with little crosshatches
as I lie here listening

to the click and rattle
of their hammers on brick,
to their whistling
while I fit and tuck

my life into my life.
Their hammers counterpoint,
as I measure the sidewalk
on my knees, in my own

string-marked plot.
They joke together
as I eavesdrop asleep,
take their sound over me

like a body
still dusty,
sweaty and gentle,
laughter in my ear.

A SWEATER

Susan Donnelly

—for Maura Doyle

Mohair: thousands of light-touched filaments,
almost alive. You knitted it for me,
a cousin-in-law you'd only met once.
Heavy with a cold, and a bad quarrel,

I stayed away from your London party.
So you gave him, my then husband,
your four months' work, wrapped in flowered paper.
Mohair: mist-enfolded sheep

      on a bare green English hillside,
      muted and still as stone outcroppings.
      Would you understand how I felt lighter
      when he'd left for your party?

      I lay coughing in the narrow hotel room,
      imagined the life I could lead,
      free from our conflicts,
      alone with a notebook in a foreign city.

            Maura, at first I wasn't sure
            its colors became me — cream and moss,
            the gentlest landscape. Or fit
            that place where woe sat inside me

            like a white stone in a field.
            Now, after years, I need to tell you
            how I gather your gift around me
            loving its light touch, its warmth, its resilience.

LUNCH BREAK ON MOODY STREET

Susan Donnelly

Not much to look at. Resign yourself
to the daunting bridal suite, the costume store's
gigantic mask of Nixon. Something that size
sweeps this block toward the commercial dustbin.
Still, people walk in to buy, or stand in thought
before their blurred reflections. The gaming room's
burnt out. A permanent smell of curry clouds
The Star of India. The Spa, Burger Palace, a thrift shop
offering arthritic tarnished forks. On Moody Street

the crosslights never say WALK. But if you make it
to the factory park, you'll find the mills
where textile workers spent their lives. You can
eat your lunch there by the falls and hear
a roar that is the river, furious glory,
an anthem flung against tall narrow windows:

Your sleepy Charles, all silver and disguised.

A LITTLE TIME TO MYSELF

John Hildebidle

Dank. Nearly dead calm.
The last of the day's bird-jabber
hardly cuts the hiss of leaves.

Laid flat against grey sky
the trees along the salt marsh
look mock-Japanese, angled by wind,

black from day-long rain.
You could call this peaceful.
Across the inlet, a dish clanks.

There's the faint petroleum
stink of someone lighting charcoal.
No etch of current on the inlet.

No one here in the house.
No one nearby whose name
I'd recognize, or who'd hear if

just now I brought out
my dark bad little boy Rage
and broke something, for practice,

or slammed a door against
whomever I could imagine nearby.

HERZEGOVINA

JOHN HILDEBIDLE

—for John Hodgen, again

The picture's silent. The moment's not.
The old one — turned edgewise to the camera —
ponders, his hands resting
lightly on a worn cane.
The other, younger — the caption says
 a grandson — howls.
It shows in the strain of his cheeks.

Behind them, a grey sky, trees
a little sparse from the wind,
and on and on in a crowd,
cemetery markers. Thank heaven
it's far away — the background houses
insist on it. Is that calm,

or despair, or just too much
to think of, too long remembering
that the old man's face
folds in upon, almost swallowing itself?
It's full day; but where's the sun?

Surely he thinks, "You live this long,
things make sense. Or ought to.
And you know who's friend, who's not.
Neighbor and neighbor and neighbor."

IMOGEN AND TWINKA AT YOSEMITE

JOHN HILDEBIDLE

After Judy Dater

The photograph's nagged me for years —
two women, so disparately matched:
shy, elegant, naked, the girl
leans on the tree. She must be chilly.
The other, seeker, questioner — she's draped
in long skirt and wrap, her camera
slung round her neck, but open and ready.

Their eyes meet, each not answering.
The young girl looks at an angle,
as if where she's headed
is a long wonder. The old one
— hair held almost in place
by a sensible headband, right hand closed
on a charm? A canister of film?
She's ringed by a cabalistic sash.
Her left hand's at her chin. She thinks out
the wisdom she might offer back.

One sees so avidly,
one knows so warily,
and not a word between them.
Stilled, they load my desk
with bafflements and evasions,
and a balance as of where and how.

MOCKER

John Hildebidle

Four years searching. Nothing but soured hopes.
I'd heard him, often enough,
grandly sporting from song to song.
But by the look of it, you'd think
this is strictly jay country,
whole trees full, allowing only the odd sparrow.
I'd just about given up, really.

Then, last Tuesday, off as always to the subway.
Passed the corner street-sign, hardly
worth a glance. But there, ample and bold,
as if asserting principality,
he sat, peered down at me,
flicked an indifferent tail, flew,
all with a grey-brown benevolence.

THERE

John Hildebidle

—for Susannah

The same tall doors,
the church, the street light.
There, I suppose, are the same moon, stars.

The calendar
says March, nearly spring.
The air's still winter. Just as it was

that night. Oh, it
was best. I took good
care of her, doubled the blanket, left

a note with her
birthday — something to
know, without name or place. Now I can

recall her twice:
on the birthing day
(how easy!), then on that high stone step,

eight years ago
tomorrow. Does she
hate me? Would she even know me,

now? The least hint?
The river's high, cold.
I won't let anyone take notice,

tomorrow. She
has a fine distant
somewhere to live in. What I have

left is certain:
the touch of her hand,
the sound she made as she took my breast.

As I left her
there wasn't a cry.
I could still see her from so far off,

that small, warm, misting breath.

FOR A FRIEND, GONE FOR A YEAR TO GALWAY

JOHN HODGEN

Most days we will not think of him as often as we say,
time winnowing up, always, to fill the hollows in our lives,
the way we return from friends' deaths to our wives.
Most days he will simply be gone, overseas,
the water too wide, friendship slipped by degrees
to something manageable, an ague or filmy cold.

But some days there will be this tug, this hold,
a woman who left her baby at a church door in the cold,
and who stands now, watching, wracked, two blocks away,
or a man who scatters his daughter's ashes lonely in a bay,
the same man, comatose, who came back to squeeze our hand.

Some days, perhaps out shovelling snow, we'll note the bland
absence in the light, the day grown dim somehow, gone gray,
the laughter lost, the wit, the words all whisked away.
And we will look down the road as for a brother, again,
yet again. Sure, and we will miss him then.

MAN TOSSES BODY FROM FOURTH FLOOR

JOHN HODGEN

> (AP)New York - A man who said his friend died of a heroin overdose
> about a week ago tossed the decomposing body out of a fourth-floor
> window of his Bronx apartment yesterday, police said.

> "And if we dropped him?" –Estragon, Waiting for Godot

It is the moment when the body was poised
on the fulcrum of the window sill,
when the week of its death, its smell, outweighed
the forty-two years of its living, its not falling out a window,
the instant that the heft of its life and death tipped, irretrievably,
like a body about to be buried at sea, before going over the side,
down the chute, the flag held behind like a cheat,
like the transfer of weight when Jesus was lowered from the cross,
the moment before the un-nailed arms flopped in a loopy embrace
on the shoulders of the bearers, on Joseph of Arimathaea,
or the second that the man who swam over to one of the Titanic lifeboats,
clasped his hands to the uppermost board just as the passengers
    pushed him away
with the oars for fear of foundering, that shift of fortune, that anti-inertia,
that every force for which there is an equal and opposite force,
that vine that wraps itself around the birch branch and pulls it down,
our Wallenda hearts, the stone of our sorrow that wakes the angels
from their sleep like a bruise that they touch in the night,
that estimable, rendered moment before the fall,
before the body lands at my feet over and over again,
that clump, like junk, like trash,
the moment when I would walk into the room, like a mute, a Jesus zombie,
like the first of my brothers to die, and pick the man up from the sill,
hold him in my arms, turn, and go down the stairs.

STOPPING THE JESUS

JOHN HODGEN

Just to see Him, you understand.
Maybe to ask Him where He's been all these years.

And if He were down on His luck, out on His ear,
on the road again, where crows sit on signs saying God is Good,
where semis go by hauling for Jesus and
shaking the air, maybe I'd go outside,
walk with Him for a spell,
the way my father said he would
before I told him he could go to hell,
before he up and died.

He lay with his face on a boiler room floor,
four hours before anyone found him, heart attack,
his sweat run off like children, his shirt unbuttoned, alas,
one hand curled before him like a cup, his back
polioed like a question mark, a giant ear, or
Samson's scattered jawbone of an ass.

I wouldn't want to stop Him, you understand.
You can't stop the Jesus. No one can do that.
Just to know if He'd seen my father, shook his hand,
if they'd walked for awhile, like Laurel and Hardy, bowler hats,
sons of the desert, another fine mess. I could live with that.

THIS DAY

John Hodgen

Today hell has finally frozen over.
Mephistopheles glides by, double-runnered, hugging,
a spark in his eye.
Today God is getting new frames,
has lost count, momentarily, of the angels and pins.
A sparrow falls, dusts himself off, spits, gets back up again.

Today is my lucky day. Heybobareebob.
I am plumb loco with luck, He Who Walks Backwards,
the one left alone in the wagon train ambush,
tetched in the head, maize boy, too much in the sun,
the one who holds on to the overturned lifeboat,
who crawls like a worm from within the mass grace.

I am high man on the totem pole.
I walk from the plane wreck, stand up in the fusillade.
There is no bullet that bears my name.
I will never be taken alive.

Today it is for other men to be broken into boys,
for others to saw at their legs to survive.
I am Jack be nimble. The world can shut its trap.
My friends, my brothers are the heavy hearts. The mark is on them.
They are scathed, fall chickens, good joes petered out.
No blood is daubed like unction on their chambered doors.
The man going through their rubbish outside
has brought them his sorrow, some vagrant plague.
They are the flies someone actually hurts.

Today the moon makes eyes at me.
Today I know the exact intensity that a woman brings
to the brushing to the left of the rivers of her hair.
When I hold her, the woman, the moon, I see in her eyes
the reflection, the waving arms of the dying and the drowned.
I make love to her anyway, lucky stiff, lucky bastard,
lucky as all get out and hell.

MY FATHER SWEARING

JOHN HODGEN

Bitch, he'd say, always, when he could not work the wood his way,
bitch, as if there were a goddess of all his troubles, grinning,
a woman at the wellspring who skewed the nail, split the joist,
drove his hefted hopes deep into the ground,
bitch, his woe, his wound, his eldest curse.

And we would gather, hidden, my brothers and I,
huddled like shepherds by the door to the shed
to hearken to the litany surely to follow, the dam that would burst,
his power and rage, hammer and tongue.

Bastard, then, predictable, and a marriage was made,
like an Adam come lately to a paradise of swearing,
the bitch and the bastard driven out of the garden
to bedevil him further, to beat the bejesus,
like a two-headed god, both mouths washed out with soap,
come to witness, come to share in the blame.

Then *son of a bitch*, and it all became clear,
a family, procreation, the Gilgamesh epic,
a new generation gathered against him,
and we were the children and he was the father
as he battered the wood, the precision gone out,
gone into the word, the word become flesh.

Then, always, incarnate, the rhythm established,
a flurry, a billingsgate of *bitch of a bitch*,
and *bitch of a bastard*, and *son of a bitch of a bitch
of a bastard*. There structure was born,
prepositional phrases, like blue Chinese lanterns hung out
beneath the moon, this swearing to God, this awful begatting.

We broke at that point, skedaddled, running off to the lilacs,
covering our mouths for fear we'd be heard,
to say in that darkness what was forbidden in the light,
a language mixed with laughter lifting up between the trees,
a forefathers' song, the words that created the world.

THE KINGFISHER

Bill Holshouser

As if I had kicked loose
the wrong stone, the one that kept
night from this place,
as if a black well had been uncapped,
darkness suddenly fills
the valley below me, a lake of shadow
and I on its shore.

Rootless skies of light fall
past me into the lake-bed;
in the creek beside me, leaves file
on currents past the bright bead
of day. There is no one to fulfill
the prophet's role at sunset, to bode
with what promise the time is full.

Unforetold, then, in the red drooping
of this late day, the kingfisher glides
from a flowering judastree draped
over the dark gorge, dives in a wet glaze
and rises. The water that drips
from his sides, brought back from night, glows
like rubies, like blood in burning drops.

SILENCE

Bill Holshouser

A tear dawns in his eye, runs its course
shining over the gullied world
of his face, and drops
below the chin's horizon.

I say, "What's the matter, Daddy Jacob?"
He says nothing.
                  The elbows of his suit
fret over the wide arms of the green
rush chair. One rocker is split, and tarred
by the edges of snagged linoleum.

         He doesn't realize you've gone. Of course
         he seldom remembers you were ever here.
         I rarely think of you either, but always
         of your absence: your absence sits at the table,
         but never speaks; your absence walks at night
         to my bedroom door, but does not come in.

I held the spoon for him. He took his soup
as simply as a plant takes in rain. Now,
as I eat, he sits alone, but his mouth
is still chewing. A meal first eaten and shat
sixty years ago? A breast now buried?

         Don't write any more. I have no interest
         in Memphis. I don't care if you are a waitress
         or a keypuncher this week. I don't care
         about your night courses. Remember how tired
         you grew of my dissertation? Send money
         if you can, but don't write. Your letters
         are wordy, intrusive, here
         where silence is fallen.

This morning I cut a cabbage, the one
that became soup. Its leaves were like a horribly
warped book. I cut out one wedge-shaped chapter
and ate it in the dry field. It was hot but damp,
the closest I've come to reading for months.

Tonight will be cool. Your absence will walk
in the house as the wind blows through it.
His eyes will stare, old and hard,
into the night. Out of the night a single eye,
far older, will stare back. I will sit,
and then sleep. No one will say anything.

NAKED BREAD

BILL HOLSHOUSER

Flaccid in prophylactic
polystyrene, this bread
I bought gratifies no one.
The careful clerk
places it in the top
of my bag to minimize
contusions from tomatoes.

Better naked bread
strapped to motorscooters,
sopping strong flavors
backfire, traffic jam, gutter talk.

Better yet
bread in backpacks
children coming home from school, loaves
whipped out in play-passion
turned to swords, to Uzis,
arriving at dinnertime
bent and tasty from the trenches.

Best perhaps
the bread that is brought to Tyrolean homes
high above mountain villages, carried
up paths that twist like the fingers
of a baker's hand, then riding in baskets
reeved on pulleys up the steepest meadows
and penetrated by that diamond air,
a second leaven of palatable light.

FINDING YOUR VOICE

BILL HOLSHOUSER

—for Erika Mumford

The forest is suspended in afternoon,
pine needles quiet the path. I wander
deeper through the sun's fingers slanting.

A spruce has fallen, or half-fallen,
trunk now a velvet of ochre woodruin
and emerald mosses, a ladder leaning upward
from forest floor to forest roof,
where the sun is climbing.

After a half-hour or more, gradually,
there is a voice — the tree's, maybe,
or yours — like you, optimistic,
like you, impatient of cowardice:

                           talk
of growth and decay, ferns nurture
their spore, leaves lightly sign the breeze,
pain takes visible form, and some of it
is healed.

            Poets, too, leave
the world's cathedral of predators behind,
yet continue to speak, though it be
as slowly and secretly as trees.

                  I wonder
how long does a voice wait in a clearing?

SKINNYDIPPING

Bill Holshouser

We were camping together, six families
among ripe cornfields, in good marriages
and bad ones, under a filling moon
and high New England August.

Children asleep, the adults were swimming
in a pond still steaming back the day's warmth,
sheltered from time by the massed song of frogs
from personality by a huge lacework of stars.

After the usual heightened casualness
undressing half turned away, looking
and not looking, there was much to be noticed
much that was different at night:

tidal lift of the moon on scrotum or breast
touch of a foot under water, shadows
between legs dark as woods over the pond.
We moonbathed on a light-soaked wooden float,

chickenfights broke out in the shallows
under flights of a luminous Frisbee.
Currents below the surface laid cool hands
on our bodies, fingering each of us singly.

Then I swam away into quiet darkness
in midpond, ruddered myself into alignment
with the Swan overhead, like Leda at camp,
and floated there, hands open to the night.

There were currents below the stars, too.
There were nerves leading to each swimmer in the mist
each hermit huddled in towels on the shore
and I gathered them all into my hands.

That's how we were bound together —
by nakedness, by revelation, games
and the reflections of games, in silence
enough to see each other's beauty,

a new constellation was imprinted
by the old one overhead, and we were its lights.
Years later now, much is changed —
those same cords stretch into a far wider night,

yet I can feel them pulsing in my hands.
The bad marriages have ended, good ones
still pick their way barefoot over the rocks,
and the cold lays private hands on us all.

Yet each of us is a star, too. There are times
I see it shining through your clothes,
other times it only wrinkles up your voice
or shakes the careless hand that holds your cup.

To strip and swim, go naked into day after day,
touch and be touched, be alone
and reach out, to notice all your strange detail,
to remember it's a joy — there's a game!

But we can't endure it, either, having
so many sexual organs: skin, eyes or noses, bare
minds, palpated by all those winters and summers,
the memories of swimmers going out into the dark.

I cry sometimes, because nothing
has turned out as I hoped it would, sometimes
because everything has turned out so well.
Often, in my mind, I swim with all of you again.

CALLING TO THE SOUL OF MY UNBORN CHILD

ADELLE LEIBLEIN

I began it when the reign of our flesh
failed to bring us a child,
after years of my body emptying itself
over and over, the way the sky goes colorless
after the biggest storm of the year, a huge blank eye,
after I had learned how the needle swings, the dark bowel gurgles,
how the body sings a litany of curious cravings.
I began it when all of my female parts clamped down
in sweat, and pleasure, and joy,
and no child came of it.

I began it when I had searched the face of my husband
who was searching mine for some slight shadow,
some mild betrayal, for some vague, soft holding-back.
I began it after I'd been warned by the roundness of pain,
been stuck with bleeding that goes unstaunched.
I began it when I had no other choice.

I take a book down off a shelf, I put it back again.
Waking from sleep I half-hear a fragment of my husband's mumble
as he drops off, " . . . love you,"
confirming in two words more than I deserve.
I do it when I'm alone in our house and say,
"When my child is my age it will be nineteen hundred and . . . "
knowing I must now rephrase.
I do it when I dream my lover a dowser,
and myself a silver strand just below the surface.
I do it when I wear black on black,
matching mode to mood, strong with power and resolve,
dark as the deepest soil, coal about to be diamond.

Once before lovemaking, I filled our room with lit candles,
laid out heaps of marigold petals and rice,
small plates of milk around the bed,
attar of roses on the pillows.
In the meantime, sweet husband asked,
"Would it help if I believed?" — an offering
in the face of all this daunting, amalgamated hope.
I couldn't bear to say no or yes.

I will do it knowing as I do
that wanting one man is dangerous, wondering
if wanting more than one is inevitable,
knowing that I am not the old dry wife,
but a sweet plowed acre . . .
I will do it because I know the discrepancy
between what we want and what we have.
I will do it in a hundred different guises,
more because of hope than of habit.

I will do it until I'm talked-out, wordless,
'til my child will hear me and move through that scrim
between this world and elsewhere,
until conditions of the universe are harmonious
and the child will come in me, and slip into her skin,
come in nakedness, breathing, rosey, and whole,
come to share with us this life on earth.

ON RECALLING THE NAME OF A WOMAN

Adelle Leiblein

I'd read it, her name, years ago at work,
innocently on a list, perhaps scratched on a random
scrap of paper, by her own hand, in ink.
Now, sparked curious, turn it over in my mind,
on my tongue — her name: Lark d'Helen,
and then my mood of melancholy undone.

This surely no given name, so one taken then, most likely.
Casting out patriarchy or naming the mother as much as the self?
"I take you, Lark d'Helen, to be my self-named self."

Lark d'Helen, I marvel at you — never knowing you,
except in memory's offhand way. Still — wonder over
your genesis, your existence, how such a Lark as this was born?
When did you come up with it, full blown and complete?
What paper did you first write it on, and was it full scale assault?
For thirty, forty years some smiling Dorothy,
some pleasant-faced Maude — now Lark.
No other name will do, no other name will lift your head
from your sewing or catch your ear in the aisles
of empty stores and churches. Lark!

Did you write it a hundred different ways like
dreamy eyed engaged girls scribbling versions
of a so-called married name: Carole Potts,
Mrs. C. L. Potts, Mrs. Charles Henry Potts?
Did you work it out: Lark d'Heaven, Lark d'Haven,
Lake Devlin?

Oh, Lark d'Helen, did your mother know this name?
Was she already dead when you first thought to whisper it?
Mercy. Maybe it came to you in a dream, an inspiration
of earthly prayer, a stay in the moments before pitching
yourself off a bridge somewhere? A salvation or a blessing
to name yourself. Have I got any of it right?

Maybe you followed a song so deep you came to a maternal root,
and your Helen, your mother, was your radical source.
Born of a woman, no surprise — as she offered you . . .
(like a river, or fire) sprung forth, full-grown woman,
yourself, Lark. Maybe she named you and I've made it all up.
Maybe the name is from jubilating after divorce, maybe you played
in fields as a child, mocked by birds, and kept your own dark counsel.

They say the venery for larks
is an *exaltation* . . . yet, here you are
a solitary . . . and with this name.
Lark d'Helen — and it is you,
if you are drunk on the moon or out on a wet road at night,
if you are lonely and bored, singing a little off key, or sleeping
naked, wearing only socks. When you tie up a bundle of trash
or see you need milk and it's too late for the store . . . it is you:
Lark d'Helen, Lark d'Helen, Lark.

You are Lark d'Helen and it fits you —
it suits you — as if I knew a damned thing about it.

I know the gurgling of grief in a life.
I've read of a girl who carved her own name
into her arm with a pen knife. Tell me
it wasn't you! Maybe your naming spared someone,
something, me.

Forgive me what your name's provoked here.
When I heard birdsong this morning, having
recalled your name when I woke,
I identified the call: Lark d'Helen.
And who's to say I'm wrong?

JUST

Adelle Leiblein

On Thanksgiving, the youngest grandchild puts on a little
floor show about being a kid, just by playing around the rooms
of her grandparents' house. Books, the little xylophone, even
a classic baby doll, her props. Those without children, me
among them, gaze with glazed eyes at the motion, grace,
and stubborn pride of a little girl a few months less than two.

Up on the couch, down on the rug, laugh, tickle, pretend pout,
she plays it all out like a string and reels us in with a flash
of sparkling eye, lilting voice, or the squeals of horseplay with Daddy.
In the highchair, snugged up to the dining room table, she sits
without her little tray, and with coloring book in hand, marks
the world, now red, now blue. Her chubby hand gripping tightly.

As the green crayon breaks in two, she takes a piece and puts it in her mouth:
destination of all things edible, or inedible, soft, sweet, or furry.
From the far side of the room her mother rises to intervene, voice
of reason, "Oh, honey, NO." In reply the baby starts to drool and choke,
her coughs and gasps rippling fear among aunts and uncles unpracticed
in attending her, their eyes fixed on the face of the so-called *angel child*.

So many chairs and people to climb over. This wheeze cuts through all
conversation, mother runs the obstacle course, watching the face contort
in choking, a less-than-a-minute-nightmare. With her mother at her elbow,
the tiny toddler expertly spits the crayon out, turns and with a smile says,
"Just teasin'." Two words chirped out finally, to collective sighs, and shaking
heads, and wry smiles of those taken in, glad what they don't know
    didn't hurt them.

And Mother replies, "Oh, Jeeze," then scoops her up and wipes her chin,
all in one deft motion. Her mother takes her from the room while,
at the far end of the table, so recently heaped with turkey, and vegetables,
snacks and treats, the old, old grandfather shakes his head and cries.
In the dark forest of his age he knows something has visited the room,
and he puts his head down on his arms, weeps, and will not be comforted.

THE SIMPLEST THINGS

Deborah Melone

I feed on your voice as on dark, nourishing bread.
Your words flowing into me are water
flowing in furrows after desert weather,
bringing cleansed air and longed-for sleep.

Each night in the stretch before sleep
I conjure you, you provide the weather
of dreams in which, reflected as in water
I see you, craving you as I crave bread.

Of all foods, the one I love best is bread,
giving comfort rich and heavy as sleep;
you fill like bread, you quench like water,
in and around and over me like weather.

In the weather of my sleep
you are bread and water,
source of my breath, my sustenance, my rest.

SNOWBALL'S CHANCE

Deborah Melone

i
do
not
know   sad
whose   lost
letter   angry
appears   always
fiercely   needful
inscribed   something
scrawlings   completely
articulated   unavailable
deliberately   inaccessible
painstakingly   inappropriate
unacknowledged   nevertheless
illuminations   obstinately
superimposed   determined
palimpsests   insistent
expressing   stubborn
someone's   growing
deepest   wildly
hidden   happy
inner   some
text   way
you
or
i

```
          i
         do               prestidigitator
        see               illusioncaster
       some               ventriloquist
      small               dreamspinner
     chance               manipulator
    nervous               hopeweaver
   delicate               rearrange
  fragilely               patterns
 blossoming               unravel
hopefulness               skeins
 cautiously               erase
  balancing               redo
   pleasure               all
    against               in
     frozen               a
      blank               so
       fear               new
        and               form
         so               magic
          i               invent
         do               rewrite
        try               lengthen
       make               extending
      faint               permission
     little               eradicating
    motions               hopelessness
   creating               manufacturing
   tentative              indestructible
  solidities              impossibilities
 snowballing
```

ON FINDING FOUR-LEAF CLOVERS

Deborah Melone

First, you must believe —
not blindly,
but with faith born of sight,

the habit of peering
at the smallest details,
knowing you will find

sooner or later
the extra leaf
that alters the pattern

to pleasing symmetry.
You must have patience —
an expectation

not of success
but of possibility
that comes from the urge

to sit in the sun,
engaged in a pursuit
in no way useful.

Luck has little
to do with the process —
unless it's the fortune

of knowing how to hope
for something
out of nothing.

Once you have gathered
your small harvest
you slip them into

a dictionary —
maybe under "C" —
spreading them out

to show their four leaves
so that one day
when you open it again

you see that the pressure
and weight of words,
the passing of time

have stiffened your finds
into brown reminders
of the pleasure you take

in the mildly irregular.
Finding them again
gives a second pleasure,

fruit of an attention
so focused
it seems a kind of love

and a conviction
that the grass beneath our feet
holds promise
of surprise.

THE OPTICS OF SPEECH

Deborah Melone

Intensity of light is *luminance*;
Chrominance, color information.
The way you speak, skin glowing, pupils bright,
adds candlepower to every conversation.
When the flush rises in your face,
your eyes onyx with something beyond sight,
I too am caught in the moment's dominance.

Everything matters so much. You leave no place
for slack attention, the half-meant word.
Your voice rushes on, each urgent phrase
tumbling over the last. Stirred,
you press forward, telling me — your glance
as you turn toward me, eager to be heard,
all luminance, all chrominance.

CALL WAITING

Deborah Melone

I had started to mutter, you were going to say —
before the interruptions and distractions,
the upholsterer, the exterminator,
busy with their additions and subtractions.

You began to mention, I almost told you that day . . .
But the call was broken by another caller,
long distance. We tried to bridge with our voices
that widening, that unbridgeable space

between us, lengthened by our choices
to remain, each of us, in the same place —
you with your furniture in need of repair
and I, struggling to rid my attic of pests.

We call to tell each other we are there,
still, despite the stains or the squirrels' nests.

AFTER I QUIT DRINKING

NORA MITCHELL

It's a bird I swallowed,
one wingtip brushing the back of my throat.
When I was nine, I spent one whole night
staring at a photograph of my mother
and trying to cry. To help me sleep
my father arranged the Big Dipper, Pole Star,
Moon, glow-in-the-dark stars
around the ceiling light,

but I imagined her drifting past
the handles of both Dippers and right through
the Hunter's chest. I wasn't sure
that she was dead.
After I quit drinking,
my life fell apart gracefully.
It was due.
To fall is a form of wanting:
I wanted more air and more time.
I wanted to be a blue parachute of myself,
so that I would never have to come to rest.

I went down those stairs
looking straight ahead.
When I reached the bottom step,
I put all my weight
where I thought the floor should be
and had six more inches still to go.
Seven, eight years later,
I don't know if I crave
a drink or not.
After a friend of mine died,
I dreamed I was leaning back in her arms
and when I woke up, the truth was
she was still gone, I just didn't want
to miss her anymore.

WHAT COMES NEXT

Nora Mitchell

She flexes her fingers,
holds her hands out, palms tilted to catch
the slow-moving earth. She could almost be
an astronaut, freed from gravity,
loose-limbed and loose-jointed.

The year she went out, propelled by pain,
the first men, packed into little cans,
were tossed into the heavens.

Because my mother walked so slowly,
I held in my joy. Because she held
her joy like breath, my lungs
expand and contract uneasily.
Because her body disintegrated,
I never doubt what comes next.

I am like many others who were born
mid-century. The big war was ten years over;
others were ten years in the making.
Our elders moved us out of the cities
and in from the farms.
We had lives that kept getting better,
we had everything.

In outer space our heroes sped
in and out of day. When they entered
the shadow, Japan, strung with lights,
cruised by beneath them.
Then their orbits started to decay,
and gravity brought them back
through seams in the hard blue atmosphere.

Our elders were not dwelling on the past.
I can't blame them for letting themselves
be hurried along.
We changed suburbs, we changed cars.

She stopped in the doorway of her new house
with the cartons and the suitcases
arrayed before her and realized
all she had brought were her things.

She drew each breath with care,
but pressed by those terrible g's
her body began to break apart.
Light bounced off objects, sound blurred,
words whistled past.
She probably saw us, her daughters,
in all our exuberance
but could not speak before we raced
to the next thing. No matter how hard we tried,
until even our passing touch
scalded her, she could not keep up.

TEDDY ROOSEVELT IN CUBA

Nora Mitchell

Climbing out that oak was like shinnying
out a deer's huge deciduous antler,

whose head was buried in the hillside,
whose haunches had sunk among the cattails,

who had wandered down to the Hudson
to drink and could never leave.

If it woke from its Rip Van Winkle sleep,
we were lost. We floated above bramble and sumac

and lived in the oak's bitter silvery breath.
It hummed, swayed, and set the air afire.

We perched in its still tornado eye
and roared up the valley, gathering

houses, cabooses, and dogs
to set forever in the clock of wind.

We chose the towns we would flatten —
Ossining, Montrose, Peekskill.

We chose our victims and our path,
the way big Freddie McAlvey

took the handoff in football games after school
and, charging through our outstretched arms at will,

picked his way through our line, leaving the wreckage
of the neighborhood strewn across the field.

We stormed the tree the way Teddy Roosevelt stormed San Juan Hill.
Its brown leaves rolled up into plump cigars,

we sat puffing, surveying our cold satisfied breath
until it was too dark to see,

leaned back, stuck our skinny bellies out,
and watched commuter trains roll shining toward the city.

LEARNING TO SING

Nora Mitchell

> *"Honey, you've got to sing with your cunt."*
> *— a jazz and blues singer to her student*

Those walls of muscle house the future,
those slabs of live concrete
fasten you to this crumbling planet.

Use that pear-shaped fist in your gut
that opens and bellows out,
the hammock slung beneath your heart
where the child rocks.

Breathe. Breathe
down the spine and through the broad belly-sacs
of your lungs. Breathe out.

Sing with the muscles of pleasure,
the ripplers, contractors, and pushers.
The head crowns, and the shoulders turn
in the world's raw entrance.

EVERYTHING AND NOTHING

—for Joseph Fine

after Anna Akhmatova's "Voronezh"

A reporter on last night's news
launched a bucketful of boiling water
into the air, where it hung,
froze.
This morning,
I walk warily over glassy ground.
Trees and powerlines are furred with ice,
cars stick in their parking places,
and above the t.v. antennas
of this northern town are ravens,
and cottonwoods, and a high blue
window that opens on everything and nothing.

We can't see stars or planets.

And all around us
sitcoms and daytime dramas unfold
in the frigid air, and we pass through them
the way we might
move through a graveyard, murmuring
excuse me to the stones
we stumble on.
In the room of the young man
returned last month to his childhood home to die,
love and revulsion take turns
at the hearts of those who stand and wait,
as the branches of the cottonwoods,
in blessing,
lift and meet above our heads.

THE BENCH

Valery Nash

That familiar scene
just before the end of the movie
when the spy holes up briefly
in a cold clear sea town
noisy with gulls, breezy with clouds.

Here he faces
inevitable execution.
He smokes, crumples the pack
and walks along the Front
in a dark coat, collar up.
The amusements stand, deserted.

And you wonder — is it comfort
he finds on that snowy bench
rubbing, checking the gun's dark steel
before he tosses it away.

The clouds ride high.
Does he even see them?
Or are they there for the movie audience
or the teenagers who stroll by?

So in the midst
of your own death you might dream
a pause, a scene's hiatus:
a cresting, icy street
of gravel, snow
where a lone white bird pecks
something.
A pale blue morning, cold
air a bit raw but fresh.

An ordinary day —
hardest of all to leave
because he thought it real:

that grainy wooden bench, those metal bolts,
those clumps of ice
under his soft thumbs.

THE EVENING HEMLOCKS

Valery Nash

Cold May Have Played a Part in Woman's Death
Providence Journal

About a half mile
after the road narrowed to a path
she drove into a landscape
of vertical white:
branches so steep
it seemed a miracle they hadn't
dropped their snow.

Her mistake was stopping
or not stopping sooner
before the drifting, the helpless
spinning of wheels.

When she looked out, all was white
but in her car
a twilight deepened.

She was in her nursery.
Tall ladies
in white shawls fringed with white
had thronged her door
to whisper a moment
over the crib
before going out.

They are stiffly elegant
in whalebone stays,
move only when the wind moves.

They tap their ivory fans
on the roof of her car.
So tall she cannot see their faces.

SEA WINDOW

Valery Nash

—for Henry

It's swimming I plan
when I go to bed early,
turn out my lamp and face
the window's dark. That cold
water of air the night
sweeps over me is stitched
with brightness, glimmering
fishes or squid.

I remember swimming at night
with you, the unfamiliar
water lapping cold
against my breasts
instead of cloth,
the ocean soft
as never by day.
I remember panic
even a little way out
on a surface of black, looking back
at blackness instead of shore.

My heart's awake
now, too, though the tall
tree of cold, my window,
isn't black or empty tonight,
but buzzing, full
of air, of wind.

And you're beside me still, as I swim
into color I can't name
except that it brings out these
lights. I feel them burning
faster the faster I go.

LIGHT - STRUCK

Valery Nash

When I was struck by swords of light
the dark corner I feared
became a passageway.

What I had loved before —
distance, bright sun, white pages —
pierced me, leaving for eyes
holes echoing lightning.

I looked up only in glimpses.
One moment of sparkling blue
was enough to last a morning
saved in recollection
like an orchid on ice.

The place I sought was deep
where I didn't write or dream
where the wind moved inside me
a kind of lapping, lapping.

*

You brought me tapes:
poetry, novels. The words
were easy to slow down. My fingers
learned which button to push.
Stop and rewind. Rewind
till meaning caught in my brain.

On our shady porch
I sang myself old songs.
A phrase or two and the tune comes back. I tasted
cakes I hadn't thought of
since the cookbooks of early marriage:
spice cake and burnt sugar.
The butter rose in my teeth.

When they wheeled me under a metal hood
to scan behind my eyes,
I was ready to hypnotize myself asleep
with poems memorized
in high school.
My heart aches and a drowsy numbness pains
. . . Heart aches.
They told me, Good.

*

When, with a bowed head,
I weeded the borders
and talked to all of you, the sun
stole up around edges of orange and gold
and air that cooled with autumn.
Clarity stroked
a sudden stripe across our rocks. Two sparrows
stood out for bread on the railing,
and I began again to read the world.

And who knows how?
When the black cormorant
dives deep for fish, and disappears, then surfaces,
we say it's the same bird.
But so much further on and so much later,
we say it must be different.

FOR SIDONIE-GABRIELLE COLETTE

VALERY NASH

These days I read biography and letters
to find out how writers grow old:
Williams' dependable energy, springing
from accouchement to gallery
to city street.
Colette's butterfly eye,
how she rarely could leave Paris at the end,
how her old friends died
not wanting her to see how much they'd changed.

Easter, outside my window the air snows seeds.
Birds chase their shadows over a sunny slope.
Before I go blind with age, I'll learn their names.
I'll learn the names of everything she touched,
taste Rozven pears, Saint-Tropez garlic,
identify acacias and chaffinches,
and dash off six swift letters a day
on blue paper,

in each of which I'll mention the sky's color,
the trapeze, and even indulge myself
with the moods of my cats.

I'm approaching her age.
I grow more impatient with waste,
and blue-hungry.

In November, she's not in season.
In June, it's enough to put her book
beside a muddy trowel.
In April, I read Colette,
sometimes allowing myself her salutation:
I tender you a paw.

THE THIEF WU WEI PLEADS FOR HIS HAND

Con Squires

Stone does not sit more still
than Wu Wei kneels before his judges.

"Your worships," says Wu Wei,
"I kneel before you guilty as charged.
Do with me what you will,
I deserve all the Five Punishments."

Impressed by Wu Wei's sense
of personal responsibility,
the judges grant him further speech.

"If I might make one small request,"
says Wu Wei, "pray do not tear the life
from this right hand of mine."

"Whip me, scourge me, stand me
in the market, my crimes written
on a neck-halter."

"But I beg you, sirs,
spare this right hand."

"Look how my five fingers gaily
wave — like the five grains, hemp,
millet, rice, wheat and pulse."

"Was it not written
by Confucian Hsun Tzu
long ago: 'The axe must not
enter the forest . . . Then
the five grains will never fail
and the people will have
abundant food."

"My five fingers are like
the five elements to me, water,
fire, wood, metal, earth."

"Think of the catastrophes
that must follow if these
elements are out of balance!"

"Seas become mountains,
seasons go out of sequence,
heaven and earth get mixed up!"

"Who could wish such fate?
Oh, spare this hand!"

"In dreams, I wear the five planets,
Venus, Jupiter, Mercury, Mars
and Saturn on the fingers of my
Universe-Hand."

"These stars ride
through the black night,
always looking for Chang Heng,
who named them."

"In the veins of this hand
flow the five metals, powders
of gold, silver, copper,
lead and iron."

"What treasures are lost
if this hand dies!"

"These fingers are fast and deadly
as kiss of centipede, scorpion,
spider, toad and viper who secrete
the five poisons Chang Tao-ling
mixed to make Elixir of Life."

"Sirs, a necromancer painted
my fingernails in the five colors:
red for joy, yellow for empire,
white for mourning, black
for the bruisings one tries
to avoid and the green that marks
a criminal on his way to die."

"Thus protected, how could
one fail to thrive?"

"See . . . there are still paint
traces in the moons of my nails."

"Spare this right hand
and I will thank the gods
by sacrificing the five beasts:
ox, goat, pig, dog and fowl!"
"With these fingers I have tasted
the five tastes — salty, bitter,
sour, sweet and fiery . . ."

"With these fingers I have sent
nourishment to the five viscera:
liver, heart, lungs, kidneys
and spleen, respectively sources
of love, propriety, righteousness,
wisdom and good faith."

"So supple, so energetic, this hand
has served the gods of life — oh,
judges, do with me what is meet,
but spare this innocent hand!"

The judges cannot speak a word.
They see the waving grains,
taste the elixir of life,
sense planets dancing in the sky.

There is but one verdict — full
pardon. And when Wu Wei dies
years later, respected by all,

his right hand is severed
and bronzed. It is venerated
by the Wu clan to this day.

ON FIRST ENCOUNTERING ZIMMER'S POEMS
WHILE DRINKING DECAF BEHIND THE DELI AT 10:10AM
AND EXPERIENCING THE CLARIFICATION
OF A SUBSTANTIAL HANGOVER AND REMEMBERING
THAT I WAS RECENTLY MISTAKEN FOR ZIMMER
THREE TIMES IN ONE EXCITING DAY

CON SQUIRES

This doppelganger business is no joke!
Not when you are fifty-five and discover
that the other, the one who is like you,
who is supposed to be alive and unknown
in Asia or Australia — well, famous
there, perhaps, just unknown to you,
as you are to him, though of course you
too are famous here if one is willing
to define "fame" narrowly enough — and
I am —

anyway, your double is supposed to appear
to you in a final dream on your deathbed,
or you are supposed to appear in a final
dream on his deathbed — the TV mystic
who's dead but because of the miracle
of tape keeps talking and talking to Moyers,
that southern guy who must do interviewing
thirty-seven hours a day, and as the mystic speaks
you have no idea what he's talking about
but you can feel your life changing,
well, anyway, even he is not clear

on which double appears to who(m),
or maybe he was clear and I forgot,
well, anyway, one of us appears to the other,
okay?, and says, I am your long-lost twin
brother, and I still am lost, but my life
gives meaning to your life as yours does
to mine, well I have to go now, so long,
see you — actually, it's nicer the other
way, I'll go and he dies, I'd really like
to see Asia and Australia, as the case
may be, but

the fact is he's not there and this is no
dream, he's here at the Mt. Holyoke
Writers' Conference and according to his
book this guy has stolen my life! Well,
not my life, *exempli gratiae*, not my wife,
my daughter, my dog, my dog's choke collar
— he's training me not to try to make him
heel — but my feelings and my experience
of life, which is the one decent thing
about being fifty-five, you have more experience
than you used to

and he's been writing about the era
of my history and all the big stuff
that made me angry, sad and disgusted
with humankind or in love with it,

and I realize, sitting here with the blinding
clarity deposited by the red ants now making
nests in each of my blood cells, that Zimmer
has not let his life get so scary that he can't
go back and think and write about it,

and I too often have, so that reading Zimmer
today, I think I understand what James Wright
meant when he lay in a summer field and watched
that hawk high overhead and he said,
"I have wasted my life."

Because not to remember is to waste
the one thing that may really be sacred,
and as I continue to look into Zimmer's book
my eyes fill with pale pink bloodshot
tears as the memories come trotting up
like puppies with slippers in their mouths,
each slipper stamped ZIMMER WAS HERE.

But I'm not mad or sad, just glad he was,
and all of you whose presence has been, is,
and will be the DNA of my life, and I'm glad
the Mt. Holyoke Writers' Conference
is no dream, and this day is not my deathbed,
but in a way my birthing bed. Because this
is my natal day, I'm fifty-five, and after all,
as it all turned out, Squires was here, too.

UNNAMED

Priscilla Webster Williams

My father wrote love letters,
sealed his initial with a ring of wax.
He traced my mother's name
with his fingertips,
then, like a pen rolling off the table,
he slid out of sight.

Mother took up knitting,
sweaters, ponchos.
She wrapped me in bitter fleece,
in skeins of yarn.

I was born with wool in my eyes
and words in my mouth,
a baby of letters,
spinning a name.

FOSTER CHILD

Priscilla Webster Williams

The day he dragged me down in the field,
the sound of hay exploding in my good ear,
milkweed pods broke loose,
brown seeds, white wings, floated everywhere.

His fingers wound around my wrists like horsewhips.
I calculated my chances: he was
ten times stronger,
four times older. I had stayed with him
three times longer than any other family.
Molly's nose was softer than moss
and he had saddled her for me
more times than I could remember.

Listen, he hissed, *open up or else*
I'll rip your insides
and they'll float away like chicken feathers.

There was a snake squeezing tight,
a burning through my body.

The next day I ripped pods from their stems,
sucked the milk, studied the tight whiteness,
the brown seeds clustered one over the other
like peacock feathers shutting down.

And still I pick off thoughts of him
that cling to me
like burrs from the field.

SKATING AT NIGHT ON SWANZEY LAKE

PRISCILLA WEBSTER WILLIAMS

I skim the blue veins,
the white arteries of ice,
whooshing to a stop
at the heart of the pond.

The pond throbs and I wonder
what is underneath.
The reeds are buried now,
but in summer will make
great peashooters.

The pond heaves
a sudden sigh,
some mysterious
exchange of carbons.

I push off into the night,
like the moon
bobbing over the birches,
content to let the lake
hiss and crackle after me,
buoyed by its groans,
the whole pond shifting
to accommodate my presence.

BRAZIL

Priscilla Webster Williams

—for Mario

When I was sixteen
you taught me Portuguese
and for the first time I believed
Rio was the most magnificent of cities,
the sweep of the bay so green I could hear
the glossolalia of seabirds —
the Christus, arms outstretched,
extending my vision to the tropical
rain forests and your ancestors.

We could see them sailing
from Mozambique
around the Cape of Good Hope
into seas that could crack a ship in half
or swallow it,
and you told me
that the sailors
and the slaves
who survived the voyage
became the bones of us all.

NOTE TO AN ANCESTOR

Priscilla Webster Williams

Some of us still wander
in lands we cannot occupy,
staking our tents in peculiar places.

Each morning we wipe the dust
from our foreheads, survey the landscape
for crusts of bread, white, like coriander seed.

We have the cloud by day and fire by night.

May we die as you did,
our old bones gathered up, carried on.

BONNIE BISHOP lives in Nahant, MA and teaches Language Arts at Full Circle High School. She has published poems in *Kalliope, Hanging Loose, Cumberland Poetry Review*, and other magazines. She has been writing poems since adolescence and is tickled pink to be EOTP's newest member.

POLLY BROWN's poems have appeared in *Ad Hoc Monadnock, Country Journal, and Beloit Poetry Journal*, among others. She hopes to release her book *White Chairs at 22 Wood Street* through Every Other Thursday Press next year.

SUSAN DONNELLY is the author of *Eve Names the Animals*, a Samuel French Morse Prize winner from Northeastern University Press, and *Tenderly Pressed, A Memoir in Poetry*. She is the recipient in 1995-96 of a Hazen Fellowship from Mount Holyoke College. Her poetry has appeared in many magazines and anthologies, including *The Norton Introduction to Poetry* and *The Norton Introduction to Literature*. She lives, writes, and teaches poetry in Cambridge, MA.

JOHN HILDEBIDLE teaches literature at MIT, lives in Cambridge, MA with his family, and has published three books: *The Old Chore* (poems; Alice James Books, 1981); *Stubbornness: A Field Guide* (fiction; SUNY-Binghamton, 1986); and *One Sleep, One Waking* (poems; Enright House of Ireland/Wyndham Hall Press, 1994). He spent the 1994-95 academic year as a Fulbright Scholar in Galway, Ireland.

JOHN HODGEN received the 1993 Bluestem Award from Emporia State University. He is also the winner of the Grolier Prize for Poetry, an Arvon Foundation Award, and the *Yankee Magazine* Award for Poetry. John's poems have appeared in such publications as *Ad Hoc Monadnock, Beloit Poetry Journal, Literary Review,* and *Massachusetts Review*. His first book is titled *In My Father's House.*

BILL HOLSHOUSER tries to play a number of simultaneous roles: husband, father, friend, low-income housing researcher, poet. Sometimes it works. In the Every Other Thursday workshop, Bill is slower with a pun than most, but gets by on his looks, melodious southern accent, and a tendency to bring cookies to meetings where others bring fat-free pretzels. He lives in Cambridge, MA.

ADELLE LEIBLEIN is a poet, teacher, and artist. Her work has appeared in *Nimrod, The Denver Quarterly,* and elsewhere. As of this writing, her first book of poems, *No Ache But Love,* remains in manuscript. She teaches at the Worcester Art Museum and offers workshops and tutorials throughout New England, when invited, and privately.

DEBORAH MELONE works as a writer for a high-tech company in Cambridge, MA. She occasionally emerges from it to greet family and friends, and to write a poem. Her most recently published poem was about food, and it appeared in the *Radcliffe Culinary Times*.

NORA MITCHELL joined EOTP soon after college and worked with the group for ten years. In 1991, she moved to Vermont to direct the MFA in Writing Program at Goddard College. When people ask her where she got her MFA, she answers, first, that she did a straight doctoral program and, second, that she did her MFA work with her writing group. Her first book, *Your Skin Is a Country*, was published by Alice James Books in 1988. A new book of poems, *Proofreading the Histories*, is due out from Alice James this spring. Her poems have appeared in *Ploughshares, Calyx, College English, Sou'wester, Hanging Loose, Hawaii Review, Radical America, Sojourner*, and *West Magazine*, among others.

VALERY NASH's first book of poems, *The Narrows*, was published by Cleveland State University Poetry Series. Her poems have appeared in many magazines and anthologies, including *Field, Poetry Northwest, Southern Poetry Review, Sojourner, Shenandoah*, and *Yankee*, where she won First Prize for Poetry in 1991. She has taught at Wheaton College and Wesleyan University, and currently lives and teaches in Rockport, MA. Her new collection, *October Swimmer*, is forthcoming this spring from Folly Cove Press.

CON SQUIRES is a writer who owns a direct mail fund-raising agency, The National Copy Clinic, Inc., located in Nahant, MA. His poems have appeared in *Ararat, Beloit Poetry Review, Dark Horse, Niagara, The Green River Review*, as well as the anthology *Witness and Wait*, published by EOTP Press. He has submitted a book-length manuscript of poems, *Alphabetical by Author*, to a variety of national contests and is feeling hopeful.

PRISCILLA WEBSTER WILLIAMS lives in Boston, MA and works as an information specialist. She also makes collages, has been known to communicate with vegetables, and often writes about the lost and the found. Most of her work, including *Poems and Prayers from the Ark*, has been published under the name Priscilla Johnson.

BOOKS FROM EVERY OTHER THURSDAY PRESS

Witness and Wait: 13 POETS FROM NEW ENGLAND

Tenderly Pressed, SUSAN DONNELLY

Willow Water, ERIKA MUMFORD

Words For Myself, ERIKA MUMFORD

To purchase books, write for information to:
Every Other Thursday Press
P. O. Box 19
Nahant, MA 01908